The Adventures of „EGBDF" the DRAGON!
...and friends

...Teaching children to read music the FUN way!

KRISTINA WILDS

THE BOOK COUNSELOR

VISIT US AT

KWPIANOANDMUSIC.COM
EMAIL: KRISTINA@KWPIANOANDMUSIC.COM

ISBN: 978-0-9980752-5-9

INFO@BOOKCOUNSELOR.COM

WWW.BOOKCOUNSELOR.COM

CONTENTS

JOIN AN ADVENTUROUS DRAGON AND HIS FRIENDS AS THEY JOUR-
NEY YOU THROUGH THE WORLD OF NOTES IN THE TREBLE AND BASS
CLEFS. TOGETHER THESE FUN LOVING CREATURES WILL SHOW YOU
HOW TO EASILY READ MUSIC AND IDENTIFY NOTES.

AWARD WINNING COMPOSER AND TEACHER, KRISTINA WILDS, AND
BESTSELLING ILLUSTRATOR, CARSTEN MELL HAVE CREATED A FUN AND
VISUAL WAY TO SEE AND READ MUSICAL NOTES.

6

NAME THE NOTES:

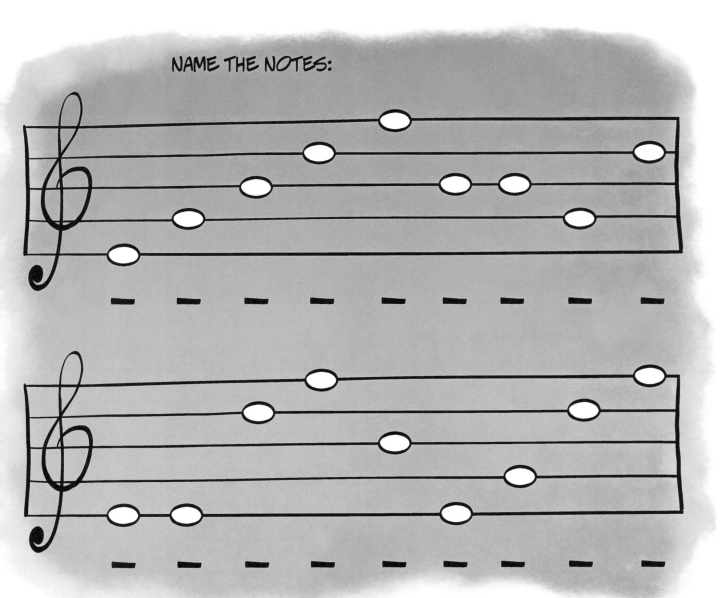

NAME THE NOTES:

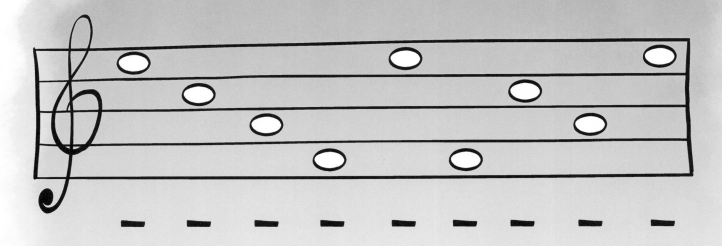

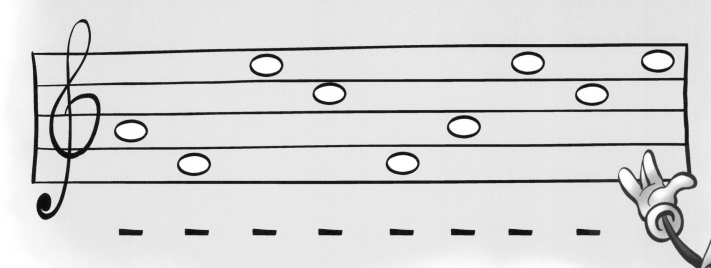

15

16

NAME THE NOTES:

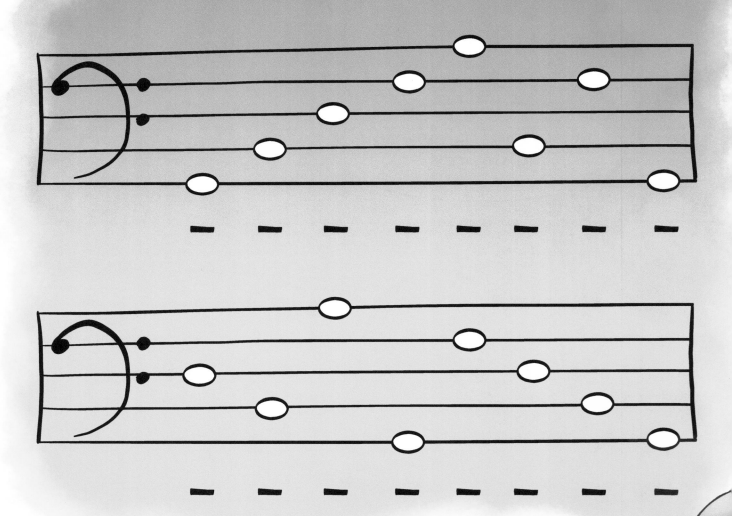

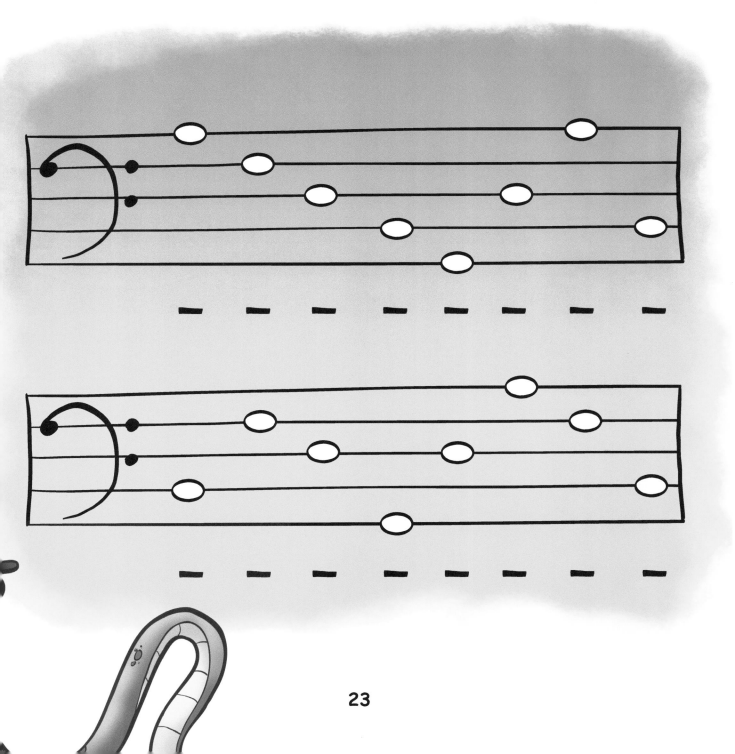

26

NAME THE NOTES:

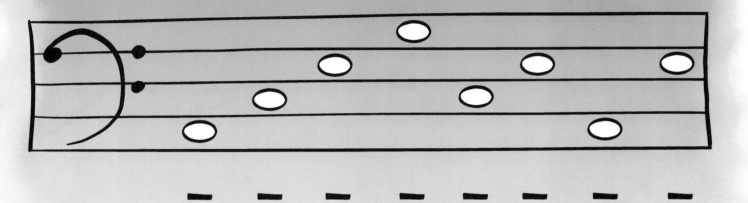

— — — — — — — — —

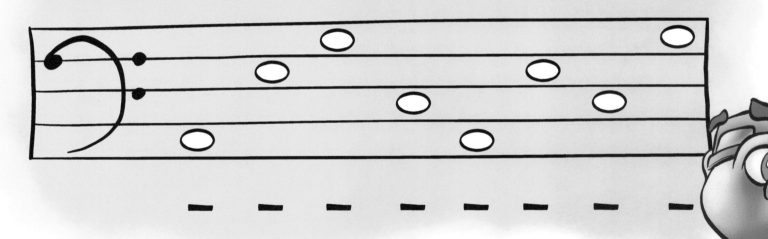

— — — — — — — — —

Lightning Source UK Ltd.
Milton Keynes UK
UKHW051255260419
341637UK00003B/34/P